"Gregorio and Daulerio have created a mosaic of stories and poems that are sharp in both delivery and craft. Both writers have created a rippling depth that resonates page after page, a feat they achieve through deft skill and razor-sharp honesty. The variety in form will keep you riveted, and the emotion seeping through the pages will stay with you long after you close the cover."

Madeline Anthes, author of *Now We Haunt This Home Together*

"The stories and poems in this collection are Polaroids that dance and shake like shadows against a backlit wall, filled with clever allegories which brighten rainy days, stretch our dream realms further, and make us question life with optimism. We learn the outsiders are observing, looking in, with hope stained on their faces."

Elle Nash, author of *Animals Eat Each Other*

With a Difference

With a Difference

Stories by Nick Gregorio
Based on Poems by Francis Daulerio

Trident Press
Boulder, CO

Hardcover ISBN: 978-1-951226-05-3
Paperback ISBN: 978-1-951226-04-6

Author Photo by David Bauer

Typeset by Nathaniel Kennon Perkins

Cover art and design by Adde Russel
www.adderussel.com

Published by Trident Press
940 Pearl St.
Boulder, CO 80302

tridentcafe.com/trident-press

For Lizz

CONTENTS

1   Preface

5   For My Wife; or, Cracking Open

7   If & When She Wakes

17   Ground Rules— Mondays, Only on CBS

27   Hunter/Gatherer

29   Wild Henry Sunflower

39   #THEPARTSOFSPACEWEHAVENOTYETSEEN; or, a Modern Prayer

43   Skate Punk in Your Nursery

47   Existentially Speaking, LLC

51   Comets...Earthquakes...Famines...Plagues...

55   A Reincarnation

PREFACE

I would be the first to tell you, if ever Alien Ant Farm's cover of MJ's "Smooth Criminal" happened to be playing, that a band making a name for themselves with someone else's tune is absolute bush. But we're all a bundle of contradictions, aren't we? It's what makes us all wonderfully captivating, and horribly frustrating creature-beasts. So, in the spirit of honesty, when learning to create art, I started with the things that inspired me with the hope that I would one day be able to find my own original voice. As a writer, a hobbyist musician, and a walking contradiction, covering material, whether directly or indirectly, was a necessary part of the process regardless if I was playing in a punk rock band, or tapping away at my laptop. Musically, I can't say I fully achieved that goal. When it comes to my fiction, however, I think my efforts were a bit more successful. And, depending on the day, I could tell you why or why not I do or do not believe that.

When I approached my friend Francis Daulerio with the idea of what eventually would become *With a Difference*—a cover album in book form—I cited a record released back in 2002 that featured Rancid and NoFX covering each other's songs. A split between punk bands was nothing new. But a cover split? That was something special. I hadn't seen anything like that done back then, and I haven't heard of it being done in the same way since. I gushed to Fran about how much I love that album and that concept with the hope that he and I could create something truly unique—just as Rancid and NoFX did—by making something new with something old by filling it with new versions of old things. A literary *Inception,* if I were to cram another pop culture reference in here to suit my needs.

With a Difference is, for me anyway, a testament to the interconnected nature of art as a practice that transcends form and genre. People refer to themselves as writers, or musicians, or painters, or sculptors, or actors, et cetera, et cetera, et al, but, no matter our chosen form of expression, it is all, when distilled to its elementary particles, expression. In this case, a really cool musical experiment birthed what we hope is a really cool literary experiment. I even took it upon myself to futz around with form and push the limits of what I though I was capable of as a writer of fictions. Fran's poem about viewing sunflowers as symbols of hope and freedom, for instance, was turned into a bit of a George Saundersian satire, full of anthropomorphized plants working corporate desk jobs, with the intent to celebrate that core of hope and freedom.

I think what I'm driving at here is that we all inspire each other in ways we could never truly appreciate. Fran's poetry has inspired me similarly to the way his high school band drove me to jealously strive to be a better musician, songwriter, whatever. So, as you can imagine, being lucky enough to have the opportunity to create something new from Fran's words was an absolute pleasure, and I tasked myself with the responsibility to do it right. I can tell you, as lighthearted as I've tried to make this preface, I did not take that responsibility lightly.

I hope you enjoy our little experiment. I hope you're inspired to go out into the world to inspire in kind. After all, in the same way that all art is expression, all humans can create wonders from the things that once provided wonderment.

Even Alien Ant Farm.

FOR MY WIFE;
OR, CRACKING OPEN

———————

It's easy for most people to forget about the glow—that pulsing energy under everyone's skin. The energy that shines through clothes, lights up dark rooms, makes it difficult to hide anything.

The glow's like the moon that way. Nobody pays attention to it until they pay attention to it. Until they step out of their cars, or the off the train, or out their front doors to take out the trash, and look up.

Huh. There it is.

Beautiful.

Or humbling.

Or frightening because of all that comes along with it— the Out There. That endless nothing that makes everyone feel teeny-tiny when they think about it.

But me, I look up just as much as I look at everyone else. Hoping to borrow some of that shine. A little bit of that normal that goes unnoticed.

Everybody glows different.

Seven billion radiant, weird, paranoid, fucking furious, goddamn happy people.

My glow's more subtle. A dim lightbulb. Never brilliant or eye-catching like the moon. Never unpredictable or strange like other people's. Never fully burned out either—there's no coil of tungsten hanging dead and black inside my ribcage. It's just sort of there. Incapable of emitting the kind of light that wows other people into paying attention.

Before, I'd tried everything. Wearing white all the time so the light would shine through easier. Concentrating on good things, bad things, anything to force myself to brighten up. Wishing I could crack my chest open to prove to myself, to everyone, the glow was there.

But now there are moments.

Moon moments.

Like at the end of certain movies. The kind that some people would call Films to let everyone know they clearly know what they're talking about.

Like getting choked up on a hook in a song I'd heard a hundred times as if I'd never heard it before and will never hear it again.

Like coming home to Liz snipping thyme, singing to herself, sitting by the window and glowing. Like her turning away from her work, smiling, her hair haloed in the afternoon sun.

The movies brighten me up a bit.

The songs a little more.

But with Liz across the room like that, I'm glowing bright enough to turn her pupils to dots. Enough for her to have to put up a hand that casts a shadow across her face.

All lips and teeth and laughter, she'll say, "See that? Told you you could glow though that shell of yours."

"It's not me," I'll say. "It's you."

She'll go back to singing, working.

And whenever moments like that happen, for a little while after the sun goes down, I don't need to turn any lights on. And I don't need to look up into the sky.

Huh. There it is.

IF & WHEN SHE WAKES

He wakes up before the sun rises.

He kisses his wife's forehead, says good morning, but she's a deep sleeper.

He ruffles his hair in the bathroom mirror, it's grayer with no product in it.

He turns on the shower, watches the water pool around the drain.

He says shit because he forgot the Drano at the supermarket, and he'll need to add it to Sunday's grocery list.

He aims for the center of the toilet bowl because the sound has more bass to it, and that's a little funny.

He washes his hair.

He washes his face.

He works his way down the rest of himself while having a conversation about the president using heinous words he'd wished he'd referenced for argument fodder when he and his uncle got into it at the home before his mother, during one of her good moments, cut them both off saying that neither of them were going to convince the other of anything so why not watch television and shut the hell up.

He can't see his feet through the soapy water, he'll need to get the Drano after work, after visiting his mother.

He dries himself, smells the towel, and adds another item to his list: laundry, and maybe another shower because maybe people will catch a whiff of mildewy tinge even if he can't.

He brushes his teeth too hard, spits a swirl of red into the sink; his father used to tell him blood lets you know your teeth are clean.

He clips his nose hairs because Sister Richard in middle school never did.

He uses two cotton swabs at once to clean his ears, can't remember which girlfriend who said it, just that she compared Q-Tipping ears to sex, just on a larger, more intense scale.

He gels his hair, pastes bits in front down to cover his LeBron-ass head—something the students can never not point out.

He pulls underclothes from the hamper he dumped the warm laundry into last night.

He stretches the waistband of his boxer briefs until it crackles a bit, gives him a bit more space around his hips—blames the dryer for the shrink.

He takes a noseful of his pants, says, "Good enough," pulls them on.

He irons the front of a fresh shirt.

He stuffs his feet into already-tied shoes.

He ties his tie the only way he knows how—crooked.

He pulls on a sport coat.

He's late, but checks the digital clock on his Fitbit anyway, says fuck three times.

He tells his wife he's leaving, kisses her.

He smiles when she responds with a series of syllables that have no business being clumped together and considered words.

He is not used to the Keurig pouring his coffee for him on a timer whether he's late or not, leaves it.

He shivers in the car, forgot to pick up his overcoat from the drycleaner.

He says shit, pretty sure he forgot to flush the toilet.

He texts, Flush the toilet before using it. Just in case.

Lid's down.

He texts, I also think I forgot to unplug the iron—hope you're not burning to death. Love you.

He listens to sports radio but doesn't really listen.

He parks in a spot that he still has trouble believing is his.

He waves to students on his way into the building, even though he knows they all wish he hadn't seen them, that they don't exist.

He pours coffee into a Styrofoam cup in his office.

He clicks through emails, returns most, deletes some.

He listens to voicemails—mostly from parents of A-students complaining that no letters come before A, no Ahhhs.

He laughs at his own joke.

He turns red after realizing the Assistant Principal was in the office during his laughing fit.

He speaks with Jim for a while; about the Eagles' play-off loss, about the gym teacher calling out again, about the afterschool SAT prep courses not filling up as quickly as the previous school year, about a rash of norovirus burning its way through most of the student body.

He pumps Purell into his palm, rubs it all over his hands.

He sits in on Mr. Holwick's English class during first period.

He eats a muffin from the cafeteria during second period.

He says fuck once he fails to open the bathroom door with his hand stuffed in his sport coat pocket—can't be too safe with a bug crawling around.

He loses the thread during a parent conference, says, "Can you repeat that for me?"

He returns phone calls.

He returns phone calls.

He returns phone calls.

He calls his mother, asks her how she's feeling today.

He does nothing for a while after he tells her he'd see her later on tonight and hangs up the phone.

He says, "Hmm?" when Jim asks him if he needs anything,

if he's okay.

He says, "No, no, I'm good. Thanks."

He roams the halls for most of the rest of the day, telling students to get to class, telling students to quiet down, telling students that, when he was a student, he always followed instructions...and that scares the shit out of him.

He takes a call from his wife just before dismissal.

He tells her, yes, he's fine.

He tells her, no, he's okay, really.

He thanks her for thinking of him in the middle of the day.

He tells her he'll thank her whenever he sees fit.

He laughs with her over the phone, but the sound is choppy and thin, like she were calling from the moon.

He stands in the main hall once the final bell rings.

He smiles at each student who glances his way as they walk by, makes blanket statements about being safe, and smart, about how they should always try to be nice, but never fail to be kind.

He is the only person in the hallway.

He walks, clicking-clacking his way to his office.

He passes teachers in their classrooms.

He waves to a few, but most don't bother looking up.

He takes lighter steps, so his shoes don't sound so lonely.

He does nothing in his office.

He calls the doctor.

He nods when he's told nothing has changed as if the woman could see him through the phoneline, says, "Yes, no, I'm here, sorry," once the doctor says, "Did I lose you?"

He packs up his things, doesn't stop when Jim comes into the office.

He says, "Good," when Jim asks how his mom is.

He says, "My mom almost convinced my dad to name me Jim. She was in love with Shatner."

He says, "She was funny like that, yeah," when Jim says she sounds like a hell of a lady.

He says, "Nothing too exciting, just have to pick up Drano at some point," when Jim asks if he's got anything going on that night or for the weekend.

He taps Drano into his Notes app in all caps with three exclamation points.

He says, "Yeah, will do, you too," when Jim tells him to have a good night.

He bites his fingernails.

He watches a TED Talk on YouTube.

He says, "Jesus Christ," after reading some of the president's recent tweets.

He stares and can't do anything but stare.

He tears off a fart into his leather chair hard enough to make himself laugh.

He logs off his computer.

He walks to his car.

He says fuck, he forgot to lock the office door.

He says, "Oh, fuck it. Know what I mean?"

He laughs a little, talking to himself...again.

He pulls away from the school lot, drives down the hill, turns on the radio.

He hears next to nothing of what Ike Reese and Johnny Marks say about the Carson Wentz, Nick Foles situation.

He forces himself to stop thinking that the Eagles' first Super Bowl could be his mother's last, if she even remembers it.

He makes himself laugh, the kids are afraid of a guy who's afraid of their parents.

He sings along with some old songs he loved in high school but can't really remember why.

He gives himself the beginnings of an erection thinking about maybe sex maybe tonight maybe.

He pulls into the parking lot at the home.

He stays in his car.

He breathes.

He breathes.

He breathes.

He says, "Okay. Here we go."

He makes his way across the parking lot.

He cocks an eyebrow with the sound of the automatic glass sliding doors, planning on ways he could fit the words "logic" or "logical" or "illogical" into any conversation he'll have for the rest of the night, and cap it off with a nod and a "fascinating."

He signs in at the front desk.

He smiles—very un-Spock-like—at the woman behind the counter, Sandy.

He says, "Yeah, me too," when she says, "You know, same old, same old."

He says, "Thanks," when she says, "You can head on back, she's waiting for you."

He walks down the hall, can almost see the soundwaves from his shoes ripple, bounce, reflect off of nothing else but tile, drywall, drop ceiling.

He knocks on his mother's open door.

He says, "Anything good on tonight?"

He purses his lips, says nothing when she calls him Bart, his father's name.

He kisses the top of her head.

He wrinkles his nose at the smell of her hair.

He asks how her dinner was.

He asks if she needs anything.

He asks if there's something she needs done while he's there.

He says, "Okay," when she shakes her head, no, with every question.

He watches Gilmore Girls with her.

He watches Home Improvement with her.

He watches the beginning of The Big Bang Theory.

He says, "Okay," when his mother shakes her head, no, after he asks if he can change the channel.

He changes the channel when she begins to snore.

He watches TV for a while, but doesn't really watch anything.

He eats his mother's leftovers on the tray next to her bed.

He says, "Fascinating," for no reason.

He says, "Insufficient facts always invite danger," for no reason.

He says, "When you eliminate the impossible, whatever remains, however improbable, must be the truth," for no other reason than he is on a roll.

He pees a little when his mother says, "I'm not a scientist or a physicist, Mr. Spock."

He says, "There she is."

He asks her how she is.

He answers her questions about his wife, work, the house.

He taps the side of his head, says, "How are you feeling up here?"

He nods, says okay, when his mother says, "If I could tell you, I wouldn't be here."

He keeps her talking as long as he can.

He tells her stories about the students even when her eyelids begin to droop, when her mouth starts hanging open.

He keeps going even after she's fallen asleep again.

He says, "I have been, and always shall be, your friend."

He holds up a hand, wishes that she may live long and prosper.

He laughs, because who does or says things like that.

He tucks his mother in.

He turns off the television.

He kisses his mother's head again.

He wrinkles his nose again.

He leaves the room.

He walks down the hall.

He asks Sandy if they could make sure his mother gets her hair washed tomorrow.

He signs out.

He counts the times his signature appears in the book.

He says, "Jesus."

He says, "Goodnight."

He walks to his car.

He turns on the radio.

He listens to Rob Ellis talk about Philadelphia sports fans and how great and ridiculous they are.

He zones out for the rest of the drive home.

He forgets the fucking Drano.

He shifts his car into park in the driveway anyway.

He forces the wrong key in the front door, struggles to pull it free.

He kisses his wife after shoving his way into the house.

He says, "She's okay," when his wife asks how his mom is doing.

He says, "I think my name's been erased though."

He says, "I don't really feel up to talking about it, if you don't mind?"

He says, "I texted you about it," when his wife says he forgot to flush the toilet.

He asks about her day, her meeting at work, her workout at the dance studio after.

He responds to her answers accordingly.

He falls silent after a bit.

He watches her watch television.

He reads a couple poems from a book called *Oyster*.

He reads one twice.

He reads it a third time.

He puts the book back on the coffee table, can't remember any of what he read.

He watches TV, but doesn't really watch anything.

He says, "Sure," when his wife asks if he wants to turn in a bit early.

He stares at her butt, left, right, left, right, on the way up the stairs.

He irons all of tomorrow's shirt before yawning, saying, "Tomorrow, maybe" to himself even though he wouldn't mind sex tonight.

He brushes his teeth, spits a peppermint swirl into the sink.

He rubs the gel out of his hair.

He checks the new red lines in the whites of his eyes, seeing if they've gotten any larger, longer, more intricate in their patterns.

He sits on the toilet.

He does nothing but read emails on his phone.

He flushes the toilet anyway.

He washes his hands.

He washes his face.

He opens the bedroom door, slow.

He shushes himself, his wife already breathing too deep for consciousness.

He climbs into bed.

He considers praying, but he doesn't pray, so he doesn't pray.

He kisses his wife goodnight.

He stares at the ceiling.

He stares at the ceiling.

He stares at the ceiling.

He closes his eyes...eventually.

He falls asleep...eventually...hoping he gets to do everything all over again tomorrow, because maybe, maybe not, and that's all he's willing to ask for right now.

GROUND RULES—
MONDAYS, ONLY ON CBS

We're in the dark.

Not the full-dark.

But a dark that makes silhouettes of heads and shoulders out of us.

And in that black, we wait.

Watch the stage.

Track the shadows crossing the set, directing, pointing, prepping, finding their places.

We whisper to each other. About the guests. About how we got our hands on our tickets. About our trips to the city in cars, or on trains, ferries, planes. About where we're from. About what we're going to eat after the show. About where the best books stores, shoe stores, thrift shops, designer boutiques, department stores are hidden. About nothing really. About everything too. And the sound we make—dead leaves blown across blacktop. Like home.

Then, it's Seacrest.

Alone, standing in a circle of light.

Going through his process. The deep breaths. The closed eyes. The microphone clutched in both hands, held in front of his heart. A normal man, charging up all the charisma his soul has to offer, channeling it.

A whisper.

"Three."

"Two."

We watch a finger point.

Seacrest looks into the camera, smiles.

Lights.

Music.

Lasers darting this way, that way across the stage.

"Welcome to Ground Rules. The only show that condenses the nonsense enough to see how well we really know one another. Tonight, we have the Kents. Suburbanites. Hard workers. Taxpayers. Good, strong family, good, strong name. But can that strength hold up under certain..." He holds out his arms.

To us.

"Ground!"

"Rules!"

The Kents are at the dinner table on the dining room set. Mr. Kent is cutting into a turkey. Mrs. Kent is helping Gramma Kent fix a plate. Grampa Kent looks like he hasn't had a proper bowel movement in a week. Danny Kent has crossed out the second N and the Y on his name tag. Beth Kent itches her nose piercing, stares at her plate.

We watch them begin to eat, ask how days were, and who learned what, and what happened when.

Danny is polite, talks a lot, but says nothing.

And Mr. Kent says Beth's name after every topic of discussion, like, "Pretty neat, huh, Beth?" and "That's something else, right, Beth?" and "Need seconds, Beth?"

And Beth makes faces at her food. Nods. Says, "Uh huh," and "Mmhmm."

Mrs. Kent wipes Gramma's chin.

Grampa fumbles with his pill case, says, "What day is this again?"

We feel it.

We know it's coming.

It's in our guts.

Seacrest steps in, says, "Beth skipped school and marched

in a gun control rally last Thursday."

Silverware on ceramic.

A cleared throat.

Grampa clicks the Monday slot on his pill case closed, picks up a knife, a fork, lifts a piece of dripping turkey half-way to his mouth, and then...

It happens.

"Where do you get off, young lady? We have the right to defend ourselves against a tyrannical government—"

"The little cap pistol you keep under your pillow won't defend you against a jet dropping a bomb on your old ass, would it? You're hilariously out-gunned by said tyrannical government, so why not just call it what it is?"

Mrs. Kent says, "How dare you talk to your grandfather like that."

Beth slams her silverware to the table, "It's overcompensation for a tiny dick, Mom. Grampa has a tiny dick."

We're losing it. Shaking. Waiting for Seacrest to step in.

So we can stop digging our nails into our palms, chewing on our lips.

Two bleeped words. Already.

A buzzer.

Seacrest stepping back into frame.

"Sorry, folks, but Grampa has broken one of the ground rules. No politics at the dinner table. Sadly, Grampa Kent..." His arms out to us again.

We explode.

"You're!"

"Better!"

"Than!"

"That!"

We watch Seacrest take us to commercial break. Watch the crew escort Grampa Kent off the stage. Watch the Kents move from the dining room set to the family room set. And we chat. About what tomorrow's going to look like. About whether or not we'd like to go to the movies or just stay in all weekend. About being Anne from Philadelphia. And Lee from Hoboken. And Dane from Kansas City. And Jamal from San Francisco.

But then, Seacrest.

And silence.

Lasers.

Music.

Teeth.

And we're back.

The Kents are now ineligible for the full ten million-dollar grand prize, told to us in a voice that doesn't make it seem all that bad. "We join them now, as they relax in front of the television."

A bowl of popcorn is passed back and forth between everyone but Gramma.

Mr. Kent laughs at something Sheldon says.

Beth folds her arms in front of her, makes a comment about how a woman walking into a comic book store shouldn't merit a laugh track.

Cue Seacrest.

"Danny tweeted the following just days ago: 'Religion is a tool for social control. Anyone who believes in religion is a pawn. Anyone who believes in God is a fool. Hashtag no gods, no managers.'"

On the television, Sheldon calls religion hokum.

We laugh a bit; the terrific timing the producers always manage during every episode.

Then, nothing.

More nothing.

Mrs. Kent raises her hand to her forehead, moves it to her chest, left shoulder, right shoulder, and there's Seacrest, and the lasers, and the music.

And us.

"You're!"

"Better!"

"Than!"

"That!"

The amount of money the Kents could've won gets cut in half. On the screen above the set, gold scissors slice through zero after zero.

We grunt and moan and hiss and boo at the Kents. Mrs. Kent just cost them all more money than we would ever see in all our lifetimes. Combined. They'd need nothing. Want nothing. If they could just keep their mouths shut.

We could do it.

Get us down there.

Give us a shot.

We'd keep the conversation light. Talk about books, and plays, and ballet. Talk about wants, and needs, and hopes, and dreams. But not The Dream. Not that one. We're not foolish enough to bring that up.

Because there's no use in it.

So we throw things.

Wads of tissue from our purses. Bags of snacks we snuck in. Shoes. Belts. Hats. Cell phones.

We're screaming, and yelling, and Seacrest cuts to commercial, and the family on the stage starts to look a bit concerned because all they needed to do was shut up, what was stopping them from just shutting up.

But then, Seacrest.

His smile.

His voice.

His way of making us understand that this is all in good fun. That the world is scary enough. That people are clawing, scratching, snapping at each other's throats enough. That this is time to enjoy the absurdity of our lives. The purposelessness. The one true thing that links us all.

That we're sunflowers. Beautiful, finite. And useless.

We're silhouettes in the dark.

Again.

And when the show comes back from the messages from their sponsors, the Kents look up into us.

They can see nothing.

Mr. Kent stands, clears his throat. "This isn't what we are."

Silence.

Darkness.

And before Seacrest can speak, redirect his show, we say, "Who."

"Are."

"You."

"We are not just our beliefs, or our points of view. We can coexist. We're a family," Mr. Kent says.

We laugh. Deep, loud. Enough to rattle the lights hanging over the Kents and their television home.

Then, "What."

"Are."

"You."

Sweating under the lights, the lasers, Mr. Kent says, "I don't know. Complex? We're a blend of billions of moments, conflicting interests, shifting morals, mounds of good, mounds of bad. We're not special. But we're not not, either."

"You."

"Are."

"Wrong."

Mr. Kent wipes his forehead with his sleeve. Gives Seacrest a look. Turns back to what's left of his family for a beat, two. "No, I don't think I am."

He says, "I think I was. Thinking something like this could get us talking again. Convincing myself that there was something wrong with us."

Seacrest, in the dark, waves off security in the name of good television.

We let Mr. Kent continue.

"We're doing the best we can," Mr. Kent says. "Some things are inexcusable. Lots of things, actually. Some people are irredeemable—maybe even more than I'd care to admit. My father should've never blown up at my daughter like that.

My daughter should've never said he had a tiny di—penis. But we're some of the good ones. I know that. I believe it."

He waves for Danny and Beth to stand with him.

Gramma just stares.

Like us.

"These are good people. We are good people. Despite the times we could be better. And I'd venture a guess to say you all are, too."

Lasers stream across the stage. Music blares across the set. Gold, silver, red confetti falls from the ceiling, is fired from stage left, right, from behind the couch and chairs, all over Gramma.

And we say nothing.

Seacrest calls the disqualified Kents back onto the stage.

Hugs them all.

Congratulates them all.

And, confetti still falling, he turns to us, the cameras, says, "The Kents have seemingly stumbled upon this season's grandest of grand prizes. Self-actualization, admitting our failings, facing our faults, learning that we always, no matter what, have more to learn, and more opportunities to grow. The Kents have realized just that. And for gaining such perspective, *Ground Rules*, only on CBS, rewards them one. Billion. Dollars."

We watch as the Kents cry, jump around, hold one another, kiss each other's faces. We watch as Seacrest shakes hands with them, the producers, the camera people. But not us.

And we grind our teeth. Dig skin and blood out of our palms. Kick the seats in front of us. Smash our smartphones to pieces on the wooden armrests.

Then we stand.

Say, "Why."

"Not."

"Us."

The music fades, cuts out. No more confetti. No more smiles, or tears.

"They."

"Are."

"Nothing."

Seacrest draws his finger across his throat. A camera person says they've cut. The Kents huddle together, put their arms around one another.

"We."

"Are."

"Something."

Seacrest's face. We've never seen it like this. And when we jump over seats, railings, each other, we catch a glimpse at just how ugly he is up close.

We go through the security guards. Push over cameras. Make our way out of the dark and onto to the stage.

"We."

"Are."

"Something."

Seacrest puts up his arms, and, for a moment, we stop.

Wait for him to say something.

But he doesn't say shit.

So we pull him apart.

"We."

"Are."

"Something."

The Kents scatter across the stage. Leave Gramma behind.

We're all over her first.

When she's just parts, we go after the rest of them.

Danny first.

Grampa.

And then, out on the street, turning Mr. Kent and Beth into nothing in front of everyone on 57th Street, we say, "We."

"Are"

"Something."

Camera phones watching.

Helicopters buzzing, filming.

People watching, then running off when they catch us watching them back.

"We."

"Are."

"Something."

And, in the sun, the heat, the sound, and the stink of the city, we are.

Every eye on us, we are.

"We."

"Are."

HUNTER/GATHERER

He called me candyass when I faked sick on opening day of buck season. Then, bowlegged and wincing, he thumped his way out the front door in nothing but jeans, a flannel shirt, an orange hat and vest. He caught the biggest buck he'd ever seen that day. So he said. Told me that it could've been me. It was the way he said it—I wasn't sure if I could've been the one to make the kill, or the one he would've put the bullet to considering how upset he was at me for skipping the day. He smiled right after that, though, said, "Should've been you," with a hand on my shoulder.

*****

He'd brought pheasant soup up to the cabin. His contribution to the club's meals for the trip. The jaundiced light from the smoked yellow plastic cover over the fluorescents made everything look sick. I crunched down on a shotgun pellet from the soup, spit blood into a napkin. Everyone laughed. "The flea'll get the hang of it sometime," he said. They laughed again. I poured them all glasses of beer from the tapped half keg for most of the rest of the night. After eleven or so, I stopped serving, sat, closed my eyes, and let my mouth hang open a little. I listened for what they'd say about me. He told everyone to keep it down a little for me.

*****

He told me he was my age when he found his stand, breath steaming from his mouth, thick, heavy. He dropped a square of black foam on a rock, said, "This is you," then leaned against a blowdown jammed between a tree fork. When he took his seat on a bare rock, his sleep apnea took its hold fast. He jolted upright catching his breath, said goddammit once a deer— couldn't see horns—was kicked out of the hedgerow by all the sound he'd made. "Supposed to shoot them," he said. He laughed after I told him he was the one sleeping on the job.

*****

After he'd gone to a knee sweating and breathing heavy enough to wheeze, he needed to put his arm around my shoulders to make his way out of the woods. I had his gun clacking against my gun—which was actually just his gun—hanging from my left one. He didn't make any sound on our way down the mountain to the cars, but I caught him clenching his jaw a lot. Once we got him sitting in the passenger side of the pickup, I helped him with his boots. Everyone else was gathered around, asking him how he was, if he needed something, calling him old, creaky, telling him to lay off all the red meat and beer. He kept saying, "No, no, I'm good." He didn't look at anyone but me.

*****

Even now I still catch myself feeling around with my tongue for buckshot in my dinner.

WILD HENRY SUNFLOWER

Most days, Wild Henry Sunflower spends his time at the corner of Broad and Juniper. Some mornings he sings songs adapted from Richard Brautigan poetry. Or "Street Fighting Man." Sometimes he carries picket signs around that read, "Purposeless? So What!"

Or, "Money is Sad Shit."

Or, "It's All Good, Man. Really."

But, every so often, he sits cross-legged with his leaves outstretched looking like he's waiting for someone to give him something.

Anything.

And when he's sitting like that, Rosalyn Rose gives him whatever she can. A croissant. A coffee. Some cash. But most of the time, when he's singing, picketing, just smiling and saying hello to people walking by, Roz will say, "What's that one mean, Wild Henry?"

Or, "That's a bit over my head, Wild Henry."

And Wild Henry will say, "Probably doesn't matter, but the words are nice, huh?"

Or, "But what a lovely head for these words to go sailing over. I'm sure they're honored just by your reading them."

He lights up when he says things like that. And not just because of the sunlight filtering through his petals, casting a yellow light onto Roz's face. It's more that he, for a moment, stands a bit taller than he already is. All green, speckled with translucent fur. Big round face, all wide-eyed and crooked-smiled like he's posing for a photo.

"I'm sure they're pretty fond of you for putting them on display, Wild Henry," Roz will say—something like that anyway.

And then she'll be on her way.

Across the street. Through the lobby of her office building. Up to her partial cubicle her bosses insist on calling a workspace.

At her desk, if she cranes her head, she can see Wild Henry twenty stories down. Singing, dancing, marching back, forth, back, forth. All the while she's sitting at her desk tap-tap-tapping at her keyboard, creating spreadsheets her bosses call grids. Doing more than she needs to because, maybe, a promotion. More money. A nicer apartment. Everything that everybody else wants, too.

She's not like everybody else, of course. Different with a capital-D. Special in the sense that she'll do great things. Be somebody. Do a thing that no one else will do. Can do.

But everybody's like that. They're all writers, singers, astronauts, firemen, chefs, movie stars, CEOs, superheroes.

And then there's Roz Rose.

So she takes her calls, leads her meetings, calls her clients, writes long emails apologizing, once again, to her clients for their poor quarterly performance despite her very best efforts. Runs her leaf down her forearm and curses herself for not trimming her thorns—sees them poking through her pantlegs too.

And when Mr. Wheat's secretary calls and tells Roz that she's wanted in his office, she thinks, maybe, she can clip them in the lady's room before seeing her bosses' boss.

"Immediately," Miss Coffee says before ending the call.

On the street below, Wild Henry holds a pair of signs.

"We're All Going to Die."

And "Well, That's One Thing We've All Got in Common."

No way he could see Roz. But he looks up, waves—probably at no one. A general sort of hello to anyone who may be watching from their window.

Still, Roz waves.

Little things like waving never hurt anyone. Even though Peggy Dandelion one workspace over makes a face like she caught a whiff of a fart.

Roz watches herself stride toward herself in the mirror hung on Mr. Wheat's door. She questions her outfit, her face, the duck-like way her roots shoot out to the sides as she walks.

Mr. Wheat would like people to see themselves as gawky, flailing beasts. Would want people to tell themselves to lay off the donuts today, right now. Or get a petal trim. Or a dye job.

Something. Anything.

Mr. Wheat says, "Yes?" when Roz knocks.

"Take a seat, Miss Rose," when she enters.

"Water?" when she sits.

Then he talks about Roz's client. How they've decided to terminate their relationship with Wheat, Incorporated. How much money that particular client spent annually. Talked percentages, dollars, and policy. His stalk-like head made a static sound the more he spoke, stood, walked this way, that, behind his desk.

"I did everything I could," Roz says.

"It wasn't enough."

"Yes, and I'm—"

"Do you know how many people could do your job, Miss Rose?"

She opened her mouth.

He said, "Everyone. Anyone could do your job."

Roz reached up, pushed a drooping petal back into place.

"Any Orchid, Tulip, or Daffodil could do your job. The position is important, who does the job doesn't matter. You may be beautiful, Miss Rose, but there are millions of people in the world just like you. And most of them wouldn't have lost this company money."

Roz doesn't move. Doesn't rail against the Wheat family name. Curse. Swipe all the kitschy crap off of Mr. Wheat's desk.

She nods, stares.

"I suggest," Mr. Wheat says, "You consider how important your position here is, and whether or not you are capable of carrying out what's expected of you."

"Yes, sir," Roz says.

"You don't want to wind up like that useless fucking Sunflower down on the street, do you?"

"No, sir," Roz says.

"Then get out there and do better, Miss Rose."

At her desk, Roz doesn't tell herself she shouldn't have thanked Mr. Wheat for the second chance. Doesn't tell herself that the thank you, thank you, thank you was a little much. Doesn't tell herself she was a fucking idiot for losing a client. Instead, she keeps her eyes on Wild Henry down below for a while. Tells herself she won't end up like him, she won't end up like him, she won't end up like him.

And, despite that, she is still what she would call polite most days. Still wishes Wild Henry a good morning, goodnight. But she sticks to dropping some loose change into his paper cup—when she has it. She says nothing to him when he's sitting, staring at the sidewalk, his petals drooped, covering his face. She hasn't seen Wild Henry all lit up like when the sun hits him just right. But that's probably because she doesn't pay him much mind anymore. Can't.

She updates her wardrobe. Works from home. Buys new selfcare products that promise new luster and color in her petals. She stays late, works weekends, calls her clients more frequently, takes the lead on new projects. Makes sure her thorns are always trimmed and never poking through her new clothes.

She has to tell her mother she's unavailable for dinner most Sunday nights anymore. Tell her father, no, she can't go to the movies on any random Wednesday night without at least a couple weeks of planning. Has to make sure she doesn't open texts from her boyfriend, Mike Daisy, because his read receipt option is always on and she'd prefer that he just assume she's canceling because of work again. Again.

And yet, despite everything, she's called into Mr. Wheat's office by Miss Coffee.

She looks good in the mirror. Real good. Good enough to give her the impression that she's a professional while she walks toward herself. Not just some post-college, wilted-petaled thirty-something. Rosalyn Rose, hard worker.

Go-getter.

Team player.

Invaluable asset.

"Low woman on the proverbial totem pole," says Mr. Wheat after the knock on the door, the invitation to sit, the offer of a glass of water. "We obviously don't have a union, but we need to keep things fair."

Roz says she doesn't understand.

Her face shifts a shade brighter than its usual red. Like when she finds a typo in emails to clients after she'd already sent them away. Or when she finds a hunk of meat in her teeth hours after lunch. Or when she accidently transposed "woody" and "perennial" during her sixth-grade family tree report while discussing the categorization of her genus.

"I'm not sure how I can make it any clearer, Miss Rose," Mr. Wheat said. "We have to terminate your position."

Roz asks if it would be alright if she had that glass of water now.

Mr. Wheat hands her a bottle from beneath his desk. It's warm in her leaf. Like he'd never expected anyone asking anything from him.

She takes a sip, says, "I did everything I thought I was supposed to do."

"I'm sorry, Miss Rose."

Another sip. "I did everything really well, too."

"There's nothing we can do, Miss Rose."

"Weekends, holidays, I was here making sure—"

"And I'm sure you understand, Miss Rose, that this has nothing to do with your performance. Whether you've been doing well or otherwise, it wouldn't have changed the outcome."

Plastic bottle crushed, leaf wet, pant leg soaked through to her thorn stumps, Roz says,

"You don't know, do you?"

"Know what, Miss Rose?"

Roz says nothing, leaves the office.

She almost flips off Miss Coffee.

But doesn't.

She stuffs what little she keeps at her desk into her purse. Doesn't respond when Peggy says, "What's wrong?" and "Roz?" and "Did they say anything about me?" Looks through the plate glass, leans against it, pushes a bit with her shoulder. Stops when there's no give at all.

Below, Wild Henry.

Picketing.

Chanting something.

Maybe about having nothing. Needing nothing. Being nothing to nobody.

"You could think of it as funemployment," Peggy says. "With the severance, I mean?"

Roz shoulders her purse, says, "Kiss my thorny green ass, you weed."

All the way down to the lobby Roz wishes elevators were equipped with reverse buttons because she should undo the past couple of minutes right now, right now, and right now.

Apologize to Peggy for the weed crack. Ask Mr. Wheat for a reference. Update her LinkedIn page, her CV, email her clients to let them know she would no longer be with Wheat, Incorporated—maybe one of them would offer her a position in another part of the city. The country. The planet.

But the elevator dings to a stop.

And Roz walks through the lobby, out the front doors.

There's music.

Like her walking away from her first job for the last time is being soundtracked.

A movie.

A documentary maybe.

About someone special.

Important.

But it's just Wild Henry.

Guitar, lyrics that don't rhyme.

"Feel yourself—finite and brilliantly purposeless, lungs fat with oxygen, unaware, and so bright."

Roz keeps her eyes to the cement, walks right past Wild Henry, says nothing.

He says something like, "Hey there, miss lady, been a while," and "There's still room for you here," and some other bullshit.

Roz keeps walking.

Past bars where she could drink herself raisin dry. Hotels where she could rent rooms just to wreck stuff that wasn't hers. Train stations where she could scope out a quasi-suitable bench to sleep on for when she's evicted from her apartment. Restaurants where she could fake a foodborne illness just to sue the pants off the chain that would most definitely settle out of court.

A hardware store having a two-for-one special on weed killer.

She's called ma'am when she goes inside.

Scans signs hanging over the aisles, endcaps, mounds made of promotional items.

Says, "Nope," when she's asked if she needs any help.

The intricate pyramid of plastic jugs twice as tall as Roz. She reads, "Kills Weeds Dead!" and "Warning!" and "Use With Care!"

She checks the price sticker.

Laughs.

Hard.

Enough that her stomach aches.

She shouldn't pay that much to do what she thought she might need to do one way or the other. Despite the savings.

Then there's Wild Henry.

All big, bright yellow petals.

Smiling, knocking on the window, holding a picket sign.

"Do Not Let Your Eyes Adjust to the Darkness."

Roz reaches up, pushes a petal back into place. Says, "What's that mean, Wild Henry?"

Through the window, Wild Henry shrugs, puts a leaf to the side of his head.

Roz asks him what it means again, louder.

Wild Henry looks like he says, "What?" or "Huh?" or "Hmm?"

Pointing through the window at the sign, nearly yelling, Roz asks what it's supposed to mean. "Does it mean anything? Should it?"

Wild Henry rolls his eyes, waves for her to come outside.

Roz fits a jug of weed killer back into its place in the pyramid.

Heads for the door.

Signpost resting on is shoulder, Wild Henry turns, heads back toward his usual place across the street from Roz's office building.

Roz calls for him to wait, please, wait for her. Breaks into a jog. Asks what the sign is supposed to mean again once she catches up.

"Not sure, actually," Wild Henry says. "Just came to me this morning. Suppose it can mean what you need it to mean when you need it to mean something."

"What does it mean to you?" Roz says, catching her breath.

"Way I see it, when nothing matters, everything does. And when there's no purpose to anything, you get a chance to make the good things count. There's a lot of mean in the world. Key is not to let it soak into your soul. I guess."

"You guess?"

"Sure. Truth is I probably don't know jack shit. You see me all pouty and miserable sometimes. Thinking like I do is hard. Takes work. Sometimes maybe too much."

"But—"

Wild Henry hands over his sign, says, "Hold that a second. Need to takffe a wiz."

Roz stays put a while before looking up, seeing what was standing over her. She counts each row of windows up to the twentieth floor, then the panes from the corner of the building to the one where she used to sit.

Wild Henry could see her.

Her desk. She can't make out the details. Nothing to see anyhow. Everything that was hers is hanging from her shoulder.

Her chair facing the wrong direction—someone will swipe that thing and use it for a rootstool before long and claim they never saw it if another employee is ever assigned to that space.

Then, "What's that supposed to mean?"

Roz turns, says, "Hmm?"

A Peony, sunlight shining pink through his petals, says, "Your sign. I like it. What's it supposed to mean?"

"Oh, I don't know." Roz looks at her fancy shoes, the sidewalk, a building she spent most of her time over the last few years but more than likely will never step root in again. "Still trying to figure it out myself."

The Peony says something about how he needed something like that right then, or that it was perfect he saw her just now. Doesn't really matter what he said exactly, because, even still, it makes Roz look back up to her window.

No one's there.

She waves anyway.

Someone up there would see her eventually.

#THEPARTSOFSPACEWEHAVENOTYETSEEN;
OR, A MODERN PRAYER

Tommy Holden @OpTOMistic • Feb 2
Hey @TheTweetOfGod. Not sure if you know, but scientists have torn a hole in spacetime. I say I'm not sure if you know, because, when I was a kid, my parents used to point up when I asked where Gamma went. If up's where you're supposed to be, we must be well past you now, right?

Tommy Holden @OpTOMistic • Feb 14
A team went through the wormhole, @TheTweetOfGod. The footage, it's...it shouldn't make sense. There are things over there that don't even look like the most bizarre sci-fi movie aliens. If people—humans, anyway—were made in your image, what do those things think you look like?

Tommy Holden @OpTOMistic • Apr 1
Pretend for a minute that we just blew a hole through a wall in Heaven. We're nice enough, sure. But we set up all our shit, start eating in all your favorite spots, using your toilets, asking for clean sheets every night. Because that's what we did, @TheTweetOfGod. We moved in.

Tommy Holden @OpTOMistic • May 5
They don't believe in you over there, @TheTweetOfGod.
They say, with all the evidence to the contrary, there's no way
you could exist. They say, there's just no room for you in their
understanding of the universe. How could you, they've asked,
considering all we're doing to them?

Tommy Holden @OpTOMistic • Jun 13
A bunch of them tried coming through the wormhole. They
brought their families. Their friends. When they were caught,
they asked for mercy. Begged for it in their odd clicking,
slurping language. They weren't shown any. Now I'm wonder-
ing about you, myself, @TheTweetOfGod.

Tommy Holden @OpTOMistic • Jun 29
We're not what you intended us to be, are we, @TheTwee-
tOfGod?

Tommy Holden @OpTOMistic • Jun 29
Or maybe we are. What the fuck does that make you,
@TheTweetOfGod? Hmm? Nothing?

Tommy Holden @OpTOMistic • Jul 5
Dreamt about you last night, @TheTweetOfGod. You were
sprinting across the starways, looking back over your shoul-
der. Your robes were flapping behind you. You were so scared
we'd reach out and grab them, pull you back. There are other
universes, you said. You could start over.

Tommy Holden @OpTOMistic • Jul 5
We don't get that luxury, do we, @TheTweetOfGod?

Tommy Holden @OpTOMistic • Jul 5
We just get to fire rockets into space. And at each other. Get to figure out a hundred ways to prove you out of existence. Figure out how to go to an alien world just to take it for ourselves. You? @TheTweetOfGod? You get to run. Make another universe full of things to let down.

Tommy Holden @OpTOMistic • Jul 5
Would you come back if they asked you to, @TheTweetOf-God? If they were so desperate they began to believe their science had made fools of them all? Could you find them in their camps, give them hope? Would you? Or would you just stay in that new universe of yours?

Tommy Holden @OpTOMistic • Jul 5
I hope like fuck you're not real, @TheTweetOfGod. I hope you're not running away like I imagined. Otherwise you'll go on creating races of Columbuses just dying to take everything for themselves. And sooner or later? One of them will come for you.

Tommy Holden @OpTOMistic • Jul 5
That hole in spacetime will be a hole through your front door. Even you, @TheTweetOfGod, must get scared up there in all that darkness, right? Hmm? Nothing?

God @TheTweetOfGod • Jul 8
Okay, seriously, do I even know you?

SKATE PUNK IN YOUR NURSERY

It's raining.

Your mom's painting.

Her belly's big, her back's hunched, her feet don't fit in her Chucks anymore. Her face is red enough to turn the paint she's rolling onto the plaster walls a different shade. She's scraped a line into the wall with her new outie, left a sky-blue dot on her shirt. She's singing a Ten Foot Pole song she only listens to when it's been lousy out for a couple days.

She sings, "I want to last forever."

Sings, "Like plastic in the landfill of your memory."

Sings, "Will you remember me?"

At my wall, I'm rolling streaks I know are going to need to be painted over—and your mom's going to want to do it herself. She's going to tell me so later on. She'll be nice about it. Always is. But I'm stuck on the raindrops clinging to the window you're going to look through while I'm holding you, when you're waiting for the school bus, when your boyfriend honks his horn because he's an idiot, when you're moving out thinking you've looked out that window your whole life. I'm stuck because, despite the gray in the sky, and the over-flowing creek down the hill, the rain hitting the glass almost helps your mom keep time. A snare hit once a second, the bass drum galloping just underneath the windchime cymbals outside, your mom doing her best impression of a bratty, sarcastic punk rock voice.

And I'm bumbling around the room, tripping over drop cloths, phone in hand, trying to record it all. I'm whispering to myself that I need to remember all of it just in case the recording doesn't get it all right.

I'd tell five-year-old you to listen, watch. Tell eighteen-year-old you to just live in it, kid —don't rush so much. Twenty-three-year-old you, before you drive your car full of all your stuff away from here, to stay a minute, get a coffee, take a seat.

Because the recording can't capture it.

And it'll end too soon.

And you'll still be in your mom a little longer yet.

Your mom sings, "When my warranty expires, when all is said and done."

Sings, "Will there be a trace?"

Sings, "Will you remember me?"

Then she says, "Wall's not going to paint itself." The smirk on her face in her voice.

And it's gone.

The rain on the window, just rain.

The chimes outside, tinkling non-music.

I tell your mom that I would, if I could go back, take that moment and make a snow globe out of it. Something. A tableau on a loop. Your mom singing, the rain keeping time, me painting, recording, telling your mom that, if I could go back, I would take that moment and make a snow globe out of it. Forever. A billion copies of the same set of seconds, minutes. Before the rain's just the rain, and before your mom gets pissed she ruined another good shirt with her belly full of you.

Your mom says, "How come?"

I point at her belly. "For her."

"You could write about it? Record yourself talking about it?"

I say, "Maybe," then dab my finger into her paint bellybutton, dot her nose with it.

She goes back to painting, ruining her shirt, singing. A different song. No Use for a Name I think. Something dreary but upbeat. And it's not the same as before. Can't be. But it's new. And, maybe, if you can make a pile of those snow globes in snow globes in your mind as they come—someplace they'll last—the rain will act as the rhythm section to some dumb, fun song you heard for the first time back in high school. And when you look out your daughter's bedroom window, you'll remember the one you grew up looking through, and then, maybe, this'll come back to you. Old and yellow, the pages stiff and noisy, but still full of the stuff we did before you.

Your mom and I paint the rest of the afternoon.

It rains for another couple days.

And nothing special really happens.

Not like we were told it would when we were kids. Like we told you when you were a kid.

But your mom keeps that wrecked shirt on all day, wears it to bed.

And we laugh about it in the morning, touching up the spots we missed on your nursery wall.

EXISTENTIALLY SPEAKING, LLC

Animals.
Unbound by the modern world.
Running wild through damp meadows of wind-bent grass.
Free.

We at Existentially Speaking have experienced all the pressures and pains of waking up before the sun does, dressing up in clothes that define us, fighting our way through traffic to get to a place that will eat eight to ten hours of sunlight. We have come home to burst pipes, sick children, overdue bills, reeking hampers. We have stared at the ceiling until two, three, four in the morning, or right up until the alarm goes off. We have also taken part in the drooling delusions provided by doctored photos of moments in lives of people we will never know. Tapped bile onto a smartphone screen, sent it away, and waited for someone, anyone to write something, anything.

Conversely, animals cannot comprehend the idea of the government, the NFL, or American life being rigged—much less have the gall to believe such a thing. They wear what grows on their backs in patterns that are unique to each of them. They live on their own terms according to their immediate needs. They exist within their natural environment instead of in spite of it. They strive to do that which we all have dared not even try: To live. To run until their legs burn.

To let it hurt. To be.

Existentially Speaking has been serving patients for more than a decade with our patented method of relieving them of the human condition. Through our FDA-approved procedures and treatment programs, you too can achieve a fuller, healthier life, and the blissful peace of mind inherent only in our four-legged cousins.

Former high school Biology teacher, Darien Gambone, of Philadelphia, Pennsylvania had this to say upon the removal of his thumbs and reversal of his knees: "I was living scared. You're told as a kid that you do what you have to, and, eventually, you can do what you want. But that's not how it works. Not for me at least. My entire life was being pushed, pulled, moved by outside forces. Circumstances I couldn't control. I didn't want to be a part of it anymore. But now I'll be able to strip off all my clothes and sprint into the woods without needing to think about what time I'll need to be back, or whether I left the iron on or not, or if my performance review would accurately reflect my work ethic. I'm happy. And I can't wait to continue my treatment with Existentially Speaking."

Anna Rangel, physician's assistant from Temecula, California, had this to say upon electing to begin treatment: "My friend had it done. I see her out in the forest sometimes when I'm out jogging. I can't believe how happy she is. Wagging her tail, her tongue hanging out, her coat so shiny and soft. I can barely make it through a workday without smoking half a pack of cigarettes or pouring some whiskey into my coffee. I want this. I need this."

Benjamin James Baker III, now going by his chosen name, Ruffy-Roo, had this to say upon his final treatment and complete metamorphosis: ...

Well, you will just have to take our word for it when we tell you that his tail has not stopped wagging since he bounded out of the CCC (Cerebral Conversion Chamber).

Our in-house procedures include, but are not limited to, the following: Limb Repurposing, Skeletal Restructuring,

Digit Reduction, Laminectomy and Spinal Column Adjustment, Fur Plugs, Auditory Enhancement, Custom Fur Pattern Grafts, Optical Shaving, Whisker Implantation, Claw Insertion, Coccyx Elongation, Neutering, Ribcage Reduction, just to name a few.

We understand that you may have reservations about our patented, FDA-approved procedures and treatments. That is perfectly natural. However, if we may, is that not what you crave? A natural state? A way to reconnect with the world that has left you behind?

You are not alone. You never were. We are not offering you a way to escape from the world. No, we are giving you the chance to live, for the first time, to your fullest potential. To become part of our planet's collective unconscious from which many people work tirelessly to remove themselves.

With Existentially Speaking, you can feel whole for the first time.

You can claw your way to the top of a mountain, howl so loud that you will not just be heard, you will be felt.

You can be your truest self.

Existentially Speaking. Become what you were meant to be.

COMETS... EARTHQUAKES... FAMINES... PLAGUES...

The house is small. Set a half mile or so off a dirt road set a mile or so off the main road.

She's on the porch.

Sitting in her favorite chair.

Tea.

A copy of *Trout Fishing in America* tucked between her fingers, so she can read one-handed.

She looks up from her book, waves. Even though, to her, from here, he's a gray blotch at the edge of their property.

He sets himself down in the front lawn. Walks, keeps her in sight, listens to the grass under his boots.

The porch stairs groan under his weight.

"How was it?" she says.

He shakes his head.

"I'm sorry." She stands, shows off the book. "I like it."

"I knew you would."

She hands him the tea.

Still hot.

"You do what you can. That's a lot."

He sits, says, "Hope so."

"Hey."

The freckle on her iris. The red in her cheeks. The crease just underneath the Cupid's Bow of her upper lip. The chip in her front tooth no one but he can see.

"I'm sorry there's no way to know if things happen the

way they're supposed to or not," she says. "Especially when you can do what you can."

*****

Dressed in primary colors, he used wave at people on the streets as he passed by thirty, forty feet over their heads. Take photos, cut ribbons, dedicate statues. Save everyone he could all the time, and make sure those he wasn't able to weren't forgotten—tell everyone who they were at press conferences, write their names in the sky over Center City. Write each one in a notebook kept in his end table drawer at home. And, when asked if he could've done more, he'd say, "I wish I could split myself into pieces, so I could be everywhere I need to be. But I can't. And I'm truly sorry for that."

Still is.

Still does.

Even from up here where he can't hear a thing. Where everyone below can still believe he'd come for them—just them—when they need him.

But it won't be everyone.

Can't be.

When his lungs begin to burn, he releases his hold on his own gravity. Lets Earth take control.

First, it's the hair on the back of his neck, standing up straight in the chilled wind.

The breath in his chest.

The sounds.

Of everything.

Carried up to him on trillions of atoms of breathable air.

And he goes about doing what he can.

But it's not enough.

A woman dies choking on smoke seeping up through the floors and heating registers in her apartment. A family of five are more car than human after a wreck that shuts down 76. A bullet catches a fourteen-year-old in the back of the head a millisecond sooner than his palm could get in between in the two. A woman's heart stops an alley away.

Even still, the people he does manage to save thank him.

And he says they're very welcome, repeating the names of the people he lost over and over in his mind.

James Neil.

Anne Jenkins.

Christopher Stevenson.

He shakes hands, gets patted on the back.

Curtis Keller.

Francis Li.

Rasheed Pilkington.

He smiles for photos, gets asked why he's wearing gray, where the cape went.

Amy McKee.

Willa Vincent.

Lawrence Katz.

He says, "Please let me know if there's anything else I can do." Then lifts himself into the air, sets off toward home saying Gregory, Trini, Erica, Walter. And Victoria, Colleen, Mark, Jai.

*****

They stay outside rocking, reading, talking until the sun sets at its usual pace.

James Neil. Anne Jenkins. Christopher Stevenson.

He listens to the wind in the grass.

Curtis Keller. Francis Li. Rasheed Pilkington.

The birds in the trees.

Amy McKee. Willa Vincent. Lawrence Katz.

The air in and out of her nostrils.

The flutter of her eyelids blinking.

Her grumbling belly.

He says, "Can I make you something for dinner?"

The sound her lips make sliding across her teeth, smiling.

Her voice saying absolutely.

She goes inside first.

And all he listens to are her footsteps through the house on the way to the tea kettle.

A REINCARNATION

First day I don't need a jacket, I like to sit in the grass and lean my back against her trunk. Not too heavy, though. She's still new. She'll be new for a while longer yet.

"That one's called 'Toward Those Bright Lights,'" I tell her, pointing to the left side of the garden at the Irises that just popped.

She uses the wind, speaks in static. It always sounds like good static to me. The same good behind her words when she was still able used them.

Toward May, the yellow filtering through the clouds soaks my shirt at the pits. Even as new as she is, though, she keeps me from burning. Same as she did when she used to slather sunblock on my back when I was a little boy. I burn just like she used to on the beach. Lobster red that would fade to tan for a day and go right back to porcelain. Only thing she didn't give me were her freckles. She told me I was lucky like that. I always thought they gave her personality. She told me they only really gave her one thing. And she hid the thing she got too well for too long.

*****

First day it's warm enough for shorts, I'm back outside with her. Telling her the names of the Gardenias, the Acacias, the Daffodils.

"'Her Body as Oxygen.'"

"'On Traveling Abroad.'"

"'Perennials Grow Beneath Us.'"

She always told me she never understood my poetry. That I was too smart for her—she'd told me that since I was in the second grade. But she loved the way the words were put together. She used words like "lovely" and "beautiful," and other words that'd made her laugh because they were all just synonyms, weren't they? I'd pick fun of her a bit, tuck a thesaurus in the mailbox when I didn't have time for a full visit, when all I could do was pass by.

She'd call, call me brat. And punk. And fink.

And I was all those things. But I could always hear her mouth stretching into a smile over the phone. She always meant what she said. But only said something when she was in the mood to show teeth, which she never liked to do. She blamed the smoking on her shaky confidence there. Despite what my dad would tell her, though, she couldn't blame the smoking for what came for her.

*****

When it's time to start spraying on sunscreen despite the shade she lends, I tell her how I scored the handwritten copies of "Hospice" with an X-Acto blade before wrapping the Peony bulbs with them. I poked holes in all the "Self-Help" with the tip of a pencil. I scratched accordions into "With Calloused Feet to Carry Us" with my fingernails. I need to look up into the green when there's no wind. Green was her favorite, so I have to assume she's interested in the craft of figuring ways she can read my stuff as much as I'm sure she still enjoys the words themselves.

She didn't want a casket. Didn't like the idea of her bones sitting in a box forever.

Didn't want to be cremated. "Too violent, too gooey," she said. She followed that up with, "Who says stuff like that? Sickos, that's who."

After all the laughing, she said, "I think I want to be something new."

*****

When it comes time for a light sweatshirt, all of her green turns all sorts of colors. The flowers in the garden are gone. All my poems have bled into the dirt with the summer rains, and I'm sure she'd had time to drink up all the words by now. Her red could mean she's a bit upset with me, the things I think. Her yellow could mean that she gets it, though—we had the same types of ways of thinking. Sad. Dark. Absurd— as she said everything always was all the time, and thereby, pretty damn funny. What little's left of the green means she liked them. For sure. Even if she doesn't know exactly why aside from the words being pretty.

*****

I did all the research. Becoming more or less a bulb herself meant that the thing growing out of her would be her. Actually her. All of her would be all of what came next. And what came next would last longer than even I would. And even if, by some chance, someone sometime down the road came along and cut her down, whatever would be made of her would still be her too. A coffee table. A bedframe. A bassinet. And then, she'd be everywhere as all sorts of things doing all kinds of stuff.

"I like that," she said. "Not really sure why, but I like that."

And, when all her color's gone, and she's just bark and branches and wood in the snow, I can say hello from the kitchen window, fog up the glass with my breath. Start more new poems she won't quite know why she likes but does anyhow. Make lists of what flowers she may want to watch bloom in the spring. Tell her which flower is what poem, and how I figured out the best ways for the roots to take hold though the paper.

*****

My back against her, able to lean a bit heavier now that she's a year stronger every year until the ground gets to be too rough on my tailbone. Until I need a cushion for my chair. Until I won't need sunscreen anymore because of all the green. Until I run out of poems. Until she doesn't need to worry about me anymore.

"I'm always going to worry," she said once. "It's a mother's job."

"Yeah," I said. "And it's my job to keep showing you you don't have to."

Maybe, one of these years, one of the poems will do that for her.

But I doubt it.

Notes

Most of the poems that inspired these stories can be found in these two beautiful collections of poetry:

If & When We Wake by Francis Daulerio & Scott Hutchison (Unsolicited Press, 2015)

Please Plant This Book by Francis Daulerio & Scott Hutchison (The Head and the Hand Press, 2018)

The one poem I used that can't be found in the aforementioned collections can be found here:

Hypertrophic Literary - "Sartre in My Nursery," September 2017

Acknowledgments

I've always wanted to release a split album with a friend's band, so my thanks, first and foremost, go to Fran Daulerio for teaming up with me to create something that, I think, is way cooler.

Thank you to my dear wife Lizz for convincing me to quit being such a damn chicken and just ask Fran if he'd be interested in doing this thing with me—without her, I would have chickened out on most of the good things in my life.

Madeline Anthes and Claire Hopple were the first to read these stories, so an enormous thank you must go to both of those incredibly talented writers and friends for all of their guidance and encouragement.

Thank you to my family, friends, and teachers for literally everything.

Thank you to every single one of my influences who, though I may never get to tell them personally, shaped me as a writer and as a person.

And thank you, too. You're great. Don't let anybody tell you any different.

About the Author

Nick Gregorio is a writer, teacher, husband, dog-dad, punk rocker, mall-walker, and teeth-grinder living just outside of Philadelphia. He is the author of two books; a novel, and a collection of short stories, both of which were published by Maudlin House in 2017 and 2018 respectively.

For more, please visit: www.nickgregorio.com

CPSIA information can be obtained
at www.ICGtesting.com
Printed in the USA
FSHW020101100520
69811FS

"With a Difference beautifully dances the line between hopeful and devastating. I was encouraged and challenged all the same. A poignant escape from my brain but a reminder of where my feet are planted."

Andy Hull of Manchester Orchestra

"The writing in With a Difference gives itself permission to wonder. One of Francis Daulerio's poems writes of "how alive this all is, / and how simple." By returning the gaze back to the wide-eyed, to the wonderful, to the act of taking-it-all-in, Daulerio and Gregorio center us in a vision of the world that hopes as much as it mourns, that laughs as much as it cries. This is writing that loves the scary, silly, wild, and wonderful world we each inhabit. To read Daulerio and Gregorio is to be more fully alive with each word."

Devin Kelly, author of *In This Quiet of Night I Say Amen*

With a Difference

With a Difference

Poems By Francis Daulerio
Based on Stories by Nick Gregorio

Trident Press
Boulder, CO

Hardcover ISBN: 978-1-951226-05-3
Paperback ISBN: 978-1-951226-04-6

Author photo courtesy of Fleur Neale of Melbourneflower Photography

Typeset by Nathaniel Kennon Perkins

Cover art and design by Adde Russel
www.adderussel.com

Published by Trident Press
940 Pearl St.
Boulder, CO 80302

tridentcafe.com/trident-press

For Leah

CONTENTS

1   Preface

3   [To Hell With] The Beyond

5   A Lesson in Theoretical Physics

9   We'll Definitely Feel Different

10   Stars & Star Maps

12   Good Grief

13   Love & Marriage & Love & Marriage

14   Wake up Dead

16   Coffee Mug

17   It's Always Nothing, It's Never Something

19   This Distance

PREFACE

_____

I've always been amazed at how the world continually recycles itself. Matter being constant as it is, we've had to get creative with how we rework and reuse what we can find around us — those backyard wrens making home in my forgotten boot, the way my daughter turns her little gray chairs into a rocket ship and launches off. Everything in a constant state of breaking apart and changing. And how lucky are we to live in a place that is so easily reimagined? So easily used and reused? It helps me see the world better than it is. It helps me keep moving forward.

When Nick first approached me about writing this book together, I was instantly drawn to the idea of it. Mostly because it sounded like a fun experiment. Also because I was ripe with drink. It was, after all, the release day of _Please Plant This Book_, and the launch event at which Nick was supporting me marked the end of two years of near constant work on the project that had ended up being significantly more challenging than I could've predicted. And so there was all the celebration, and all the flailing of arms, and all the clinking of glasses one expects at these things, and there was Nick with this exciting new idea that felt like a deep, fresh breath. And so it was a quick yes, knowing still that I was already bent on writing a new full-length with my pal, Scott, who had illus-

trated the first two collections, and that the days were already feeling squeezed. But knowing, too, that I had just recently trashed a near-finished manuscript, I thought this might be a good reset. Something to cleanse the palate, which might help me venture into places I'd not yet explored. It would be fun. It would be new.

Scott died a month and a half later, and scared of my grief as I was, I wrapped myself in tributes and benefits, hiding from the sad reality. There was no new writing. There was no forward.

The poems eventually came back, though not quickly, and not without pain. At first they were mostly pieces for the book I'd hoped to write with Scott, which had changed considerably in tone. But then the "cover" poems started falling out, too, different than I'd expected, and feeling less like a palate cleanse and more like a mental one. I found myself in places I'd not expected, inside Nick's far-out stories of space travel and superheroes. The huge and unreal suddenly became small and intimate, and as I bent his ideas every which way, the root became the focus. Looking over them now, I'm finding that this project, this sharing of love and grief, helped open me back up and see the world in a way I had wanted to before things all crashed apart.

And so here we remember what we already know — that art can be used like a tool, like medicine, to meet us where we are, to help transform us into what we hope to be, or at the very least, understand how we got here. And so here is *With a Difference*, its title taken from Shakespeare's *Hamlet*, Ophelia's own reminder that we might find communal remedies for our individual struggles. This is a collection of covers by two friends, sharing their work, their love, their grief with one another, and now with you, that you might swallow it up and feel different for it. Better.

It's saying, please, I have created this thing to help find hope for myself.

It's saying, please, use it how you can to find hope of your own.

[TO HELL WITH] THE BEYOND

"Turn your back to the afterlife.
Kick dust into the eyes of it all."
                          - Scott Hutchison

You can come in
with your darkness fluttering around
you like flies
on the dead thing,
or shrouded in whichever
style of sadness is in season.

You can sulk in through the door,
quiet toward the corner,
or louder now, if you're the type
to wrap yourself
in noise.

That's fine. Come
with your noise.

You are welcome
with your tension, weakness,
all sunken-eyed and weary,
hauling that sack of sorrows,
hidden fears,
and flightless birds.

Bring it all. Whatever
you can't let go of,
whatever won't let go of you.

Come how you can.
Anything is okay.
Just don't spiral off
out there, head in your hands,
drifting faster and faster
toward the exit.

Forget about the beyond
for awhile.
All of that can wait.

A LESSON IN THEORETICAL PHYSICS

I don't know what keeps me here
in this dawning kitchen
each day, turning over
the cardboard backing
of a spent sketchpad
sent from far away
by a friend I loved, who,
a little while before
his mind swept him out,
labored over the thing,
used his thumb to smudge bits
of penciled patterns,
holding it now in my hands
how he might've
and asking,
out loud sometimes,
  where'd you go?

  *

Never bright enough
for upper science,
I tweezed mouse teeth out of owl shit
while the smart kids learned
about constants and laws
I wouldn't understand yet,
not until the puncture wounds
of loss let the want seep in,
the need to understand
how someone, *everyone*,
can cease.

*

If you believe
the scientists,
we probably fill
the same spaces,
us and everyone
who ever flickered out.
And sure, the details are confusing,
something about energy,
a simple difference in vibrational speed
the only thing separating us
from the others who are probably
in our spaces, [their spaces, too]
right now,
all of us
sucking the same air,
tracking dirt across the carpet,
rifling through each others' shit,
missing everything that is
all at once everywhere.

*

Pulling out of the driveway last night,
a wedged stone in the tread
of my tire kept with me
for awhile,
clicking a little rhythm
that changed pitch with speed
as I wove the backroads
toward the highway, where
it disappeared into the drone.

> When I got where I was going
> it was gone

WE'LL DEFINITELY FEEL DIFFERENT

It's true that, the night before
my confirmation, I probably crammed
too much spaghetti down quick,
bothered my friend's mom
to let him out past dark,
and when she said no, probably
spent the night alone
watching *Seinfeld* reruns,
probably a little nervous for
the day ahead,
definitely not studying
a bit of what I was told to learn
to help make sense of my *new life*,
a bundle of khaki and blue-blazered nerves
that next day, which ended unremarkably,
probably, or enough so at least
that all I've held onto is the way
my sweaty hands turned
the Bible pages see-through
and nothing else.

Later on that year
the neighbors stocked cans of food
and gassed up generators
for the end of the world,
then waited while Dick Clark
counted us down to the nothing,
and when it didn't happen,
the little hands still clicking forward,
we crossed over
into midnight
exactly the same
as we'd entered—
         scared, silly, unprepared.

STARS & STAR MAPS

For a long time I believed
in all of it—
       the chants and robes,
       candlelit histories
       thick-spined
       with obedience,
       all the bread and blood
       foreverness that felt
       so huge and old.

       Then for awhile,
       nothing.

But now, switching off
the patio lights
everything gets big again,
bright blipped and filament,
so goddamn wide
there's no telling
how far it goes, and I remember
people used to pray
to this, gave it names,
taught it shit
they'd pretend to learn
right back from it.

 Last week, wine drunk
and lying in the backyard,
watching March
splatter-paint the sky silver,
I felt it,
the size if nothing else,
and all those stars,
burning for nothing.
The grass around me swayed

and my skin knew before I did
how alive this all is,
     and how simple.

GOOD GRIEF

So what
if the past jumps out
in front of us,
does flips and kicks,
flashes those gapped-up baby teeth,
seems safer
than the bitter road ahead
stretching and curving
out of sight?

Put your younger selves to rest.
Mourn them if you have to,
but call them on their bullshit,
leave them and their innocence
in photo books and
sepia-toned graves.

Don't let them block what's still to come.
            We needn't piss in the wind.

LOVE & MARRIAGE & LOVE & MARRIAGE

For what more
could we ask
but to live
in late summer's
weather-roughed skin,
rolling filthy
in the backyard, the lawn
gone to seed?

WAKE UP DEAD

I'm a ghost all night,
hovering above her crib
in this four-watt bedroom,
all seafoam, pink, and *Fancy Nancy,*
strained eyes scanning
for evidence of life,
the twitch of a finger or lip,
the rise and fall of her onesie
(tonight's selection, a feline number with paws for feet),
holding my breath for as long as I can
and standing perfectly still
to better catch her vitals
before returning to my tossing
sleepless panic of *what-ifs*
and bits of a nightmare where I'm running
down the hallway toward a scream
I can't reach,
which rockets me back up
and down the *real* hall
toward the *real* room
to start the haunt again.

And of course I know my fear
is common,
but common, too, are the catastrophes.
Different types, maybe,
and individually rare, sure,
but all of these slight chances
are enough to keep my nightly pacing
nightly,
each morning a red-eyed sleepdrive
past two children's hospitals,
finally collapsing into my desk to smile
at the bright photo
of a perfectly healthy girl.

We parents are modern cliches—
each talks of our haunting
fingers under noses
feeling for airflow
and stray limbs tucked
back under blankets.

Our squeaky boards and errant yawns
become what they'll grow to know as ghosts,
the ones who each night float above them,

whispering, *stay here*,

like every night before, *stay here*,

and so many nights to come, *stay here*.

COFFEE MUG

Wiping each brown ring
from the top of my desk
while the kids go
all exhaust burn and vape puff
into new warmth,
I have to laugh
at this stock photo
I'm becoming—
      tote bag lunches
      and book recs scattered
      on the floorboard of my Outback,
      NPR and step counts,
      jitter mornings, scotch sleeps,
      early grays and so scattered
      that the calm never quite sinks,
      even as the long drunk of summer
      pours June into July,
      quick months that blink
      into late August's heat—
        a new crop
           and more English.

IT'S ALWAYS NOTHING,
IT'S NEVER SOMETHING

———————————

On the first inhalation
there will be mostly rotten bits
of bad sex and misplaced love,
that awful job and what little
comes away compared
to all that's lost,
that asshole boss,
that too-tight parking spot.
Wanting to be rid of this,
we'll focus on it more
at first.

The exhale, then, nothing
but stale coffee, a little restless,
a little bitter.

The next inhalation, slower now,
will go a little deeper,
a little inward,
the awkward pasts
holding our night watches,
the constant scrolling,
all the needing for stuff
later boxed or lost,
how cruel we are
to ourselves.

Upon the exhalation, though
may come a feeling
of release.

A few more and the forget begins.

More still and the breath itself
becomes a state of being,
another part of the great communal
sigh, eyes closed,
the mental line of sight
should run
the way a crack along the ceiling
first follows straight
down the crease between panels
of drywall
before splitting off and going
wild, whichever way
across the landscape of false sky,
which, ultimately, we should
think past, zooming out
over everything, and feeling,
from this distance,
how tiny.

On the final exhalation there will be
nothing, simply.

Here is the void,
and we will float in it,
holding on for another
second.

And another second.

And another.

THIS DISTANCE

Let's click on
the long zoom,
fuck off for awhile
and head out
past the noise,
the danger,
the mess.

I want to be your Wonka.
I want to get you high.
Blow that elevator
straight through the glass,
full speed up
and out
to where it's nothing
but bluegreen colorwash
and deadass quiet.

Imagine it, yeah?
All the way up there,
what it must look like.
Such peace.
Understanding.
Everything turning,
calm and easy,
and from far enough up
you won't have to hear
the opinions,
catch the updates,
listen to the nonsense
from all those intolerant shits

who kept you smaller
than you should be,
less you to leave
more room for them.

They'll all just be part
of the big spin.

From up here it'll be simple.
From this distance it'll be ok.

Notes

The original stories that inspired these poems can be found in these books. Both were written by Nick Gregorio. Both are wonderful.

Good Grief (Maudlin House, 2017)

This Distance (Maudlin House, 2018)

Toho Journal - "We'll Definitely Feel Different" Fall 2019.

The epigraph in [To Hell With] The Beyond was taken from the following source:

Hutchison, Scott John. "A Good Reason to Grow Old." *Owl John*, Atlantic Records, 2014.

Acknowledgments

A whole bucketful of thanks to Nick Gregorio for welcoming me into this wonderful project. All the love and thanks to my wife, Leah, and my family for their constant support (and patience). A bouquet of thanks tied with a big purple bow to Rich Appel for helping me twist and turn these words into what some might generously call poetry. This book would most definitely not exist without him.

More thanks, too, to the friends, mentors, and guides who served as beacons of light.

Finally, thanks to you, reader. You're a dream.

About the Author

Francis Daulerio is the author of two collaborative collections of poetry and art, both featuring the illustrations of Scott Hutchison. Now in its second edition, his 2015 debut, If & When We Wake, chronicles the process of healing after loss. His second collection, a 50th anniversary reinterpretation of Richard Brautigan's Please Plant This Book, benefits the American Foundation for Suicide Prevention. Francis is a mental health advocate and a proud supporter of the Tiny Changes charity organization. He lives outside Philadelphia with his wife, children, and a small herd of deer.

More information can be found at www.FrancisDaulerio.com